The Beginner`s Stock

Stock

Things you need to know before stepping into the stock market.

Akash Patel

DEDICATION

This is presented as a work of non-fiction and dedicated to nobody.

CONTENTS

1 INTRODUCTION

Even in today`s time if you go to your neighbor, friends, or relatives and ask them about stock market investment, or what they think about the stock market, then many of them will discourage you or stop you from investing in stocks. Even nowadays many people think that there is no logic in the stock market, if anyone earns or gets successful through the stock market then it's just by its luck. But that's not true, today many successful people (like Warren Buffett, Rakesh Jhunjhunwala, etc.) made their fortune just by investing in the stock market, and imagine that is it possible that just by luck a person can become 4th richest person (Warren Buffett) in the world. Surely No, or if we talk about Rakesh Jhunjhunwala, who is the 48th richest person in India, has also made his fortune through the stock market.

Nowadays many of us want to make money through the stock market when we see people earning through it. So, what many of us do is that we step into the stock market without any knowledge or study and face losses at the very first try and become discouraged. So, the first thing which we have to do before investing in stocks is to learn and then invest. Always try to avoid random advice from different people, who say that, invest in this stock or that without any information. As, when it comes to investment, everyone wants to be careful and move because after all, it is about money.

Now let's see what the stock market is or how it works.

A company needs funds for the expansion and growth of its business. There are different ways to raise money, like from angel investors or venture capitals, from banks or institution loans, from the public through the stock market, etc.

There are two ways for a company to raise money.
One is Debt Financing and the other is Equity Financing.

Debt Financing, Debt means a loan, so debt financing means taking a loan for business growth.
The money taken from debt financing is to be returned after some time from where the company took it and also has to give interest on that money.

Equity Financing, Equity means giving a part of ownership to someone in return for money.
At the same time, when a company raises money through equity financing, the company didn't need to return that money and didn't need to pay interest on it. In return, the company gives a stake (a part) to the investors from which the company gets the funds and the investor becomes a partner of that company. So

when a company raises funds from the stock market, it is called equity financing.

The stock market is a platform for investors where anyone, whether rich or poor, can buy shares and become a partner in that company.
Similarly stock market is a platform for companies, from which companies can raise funds from the public.

So, whatever company is in the stock market, they have raised funds from the public and in return, they have given partnership to the public and such companies are called Public Companies.
When the company first raises funds from the public, it is called IPO (Initial Public Offering). You get a partnership in the company in the proportion of shares that you buy.
In an IPO, the company together with the investment bank decides the price or price band of the share. Normally the IPO is open for 3 days and during these 3 days, the investor has to subscribe to the shares of the company and thereafter allotment of shares begins. In an IPO, you can only buy shares from the company, not sell them.
To sell a share, you have to wait until stock gets listed on the stock exchange. A few days after, when the share is allotted in IPO, the stock gets listed on the stock exchange and after getting listed, you can sell the shares purchased in IPO at the stock exchange. When you sell your shares, the partnership of that company also gets transferred to a new investor who bought shares from you.
In this way, shares issued by the company in the IPO,

exchanges between people on the stock exchange.

The transactions that take place on the stock exchange are between investors and do not include the company. When you buy shares in an IPO, you buy shares directly from the company, but the same when you buy shares on the stock exchange, then you buy shares from another investor.

Stock exchange brings together those who want to buy shares and those who want to sell, and it is all online, so you can buy and sell shares from anywhere. Stock exchange uses an automatic order matching system, when the order of the buyer and seller matches, the transaction gets completed.

We need a Demat account as it is compulsory to invest in the stock market whether we want to buy an IPO or shares. Demat means dematerialization means converting and storing physical share certificates into digital form. Stock brokerage firms like Zerodha, 5paisa, etc. work as mediators where we have to open Demat accounts so that we can buy/ sell shares and in return for this we have to pay some charge to these brokerage firms, and this charge is known as brokerage fees.

Demat account is used to keep stocks in the same way we keep our money in a bank saving account. With the Demat account, we also need a trading account because the trading account is used to buy and sell stocks and the stocks which we purchase are stored in the Demat account. We need basic documents like PAN card, address proof, bank proof, etc. to open

Demat and trading account. When we open a Demat account we get a trading account with it so, we do not need to open a trading account separately.

After opening
Demat account, we can sell shares in 3 ways.

• Using a   mobile app of the   stock brokerage firm.
• Using website or software of stock brokerage firm.
• Directly calling stock brokerage firms and ask them t o buy or sell shares.
With some brokerage firms (like Zerodha) we do not need to maintain a   minimum balance in   the trading account, so by opening an account with such a brokerage firm, we can invest in the   stock market with a   small amount also. Always open a Demat account with a brokerage firm whose service is good and has low brokerage charge and is affordable.
We can easily sell and buy stock on the stock exchange at the   time of the stock exchange ie 9:00 am to 3:30 pm through your tra ding account.

India`s Stock Exchange-

India has two main stock exchanges: NSE and BSE.
NSE: National Stock Exchange
BSE: Bombay Stock Exchange
There are over 1600 companies listed on NSE and over 5500 companies listed on BSE.
You are not able to track all these companies' stocks, so to know the condition of the stock market indices are made which is Sensex and Nifty.

SENSEX is BSE's main index.

SENSEX is made up of 30 well-established and well-tracked companies of different sectors and the movement of SENSEX depends on the performance of these 30 companies' stocks included in SENSEX.

SENSEX means sensitive + index,

On the other hand, NIFTY, the main index of NSE, consists of 50 well-established and companies with a good track record. The movements of the NIFTY depend on the performance of these 50 stocks included in NIFTY.

NIFTY means Nifty + Fifty.

In the Nifty, there are 30 companies that are in the Sensex and with them, another 20 well-established companies are included.

The companies which are involved in Nifty and Sensex are selected from almost all the different sectors like Pharma, IT, Energy, Telecom, financial services, etc., and they are leading companies in their respective sectors.

In this way, different sectors are covered in Nifty and Sensex. That is why the performance of the Nifty and the Sensex is considered to be the performance of the stock market. When Sensex and Nifty increase, we say that the stock market is performing well and when Sensex and Nifty fall, we say that the stock market is performing poorly.

Trading and investing-

Many people think that trading and investing mean the same. But it is not so.

In trading, the share is held for a few seconds to a few months.

Some Types of Trading are

- Scalp Trading
- Intraday Trading
- Swing Trading
- Position Trading.

- In scalp trading, the stock is held for a few seconds to a few minutes.

- In intraday trading, you have to sell the shares on the same day. This is the most popular way of trading.

- In swing trading, the stock is held for a few days to a few weeks.

- In position trading, the stock is held for a few months.

- Apart from these, another way of trading is BTST- Buy Today, Sell Tomorrow.

Traders try to make money from the price movement of stocks. Traders use technical analysis for their stock analysis. In technical analysis, the trader analyzes price and volume with the help of charts, and then the supply and demand of the stock. Those who do trading are called traders.

Those who invest, are called Investors. Investments are made for the long term i.e. for more than one year. Investors use buy and hold approaches and prefer to keep the stock hold for years.

Investors view investing in a company as a partnership and stay in those shares for years. Investors always think like businessmen, the way businessmen understand a business and go through it. Similarly, investors also understand a company and closely follow the company.

Fundamental analysis is followed for company analysis in Investing. Investing involves two things, Value Investing and Growth Investing.

As we have seen, the focus of the traders is on the price and volume of the stock, while the investor is focused on the fundamentals of the company.

In the long term, the price of the stock follows the growth of the company, which is why investors conduct a fundamental analysis of the company. In the same short term, there is a lot of volatility, that's why traders do Technical analysis because of stock price and volume analysis.

Taxation in Stock Market –

So now let's talk about taxation. In trading, the shares are held for a short term, so if you hold the stock for a period of less than 1 year, then you will be charged Short Term Capital Gains Tax on profits, which is probably 15% now.

But this rule does not apply to intraday trading. If you do intraday trading then you have to pay tax on your profit according to your tax slab.

For Ex- If you come in a 20% tax slab for your income, then you have to pay 20% tax on your profit. This means the tax on the profit you earn from intraday trading will be according to your income tax.

Investors hold the stock for many years. If you hold the stock for a period of more than 1 year, you get rid of the capital gain tax. So being an investor is also an advantage. But it has some exception which is that, if you earn around 10 lakhs by investing in the stock market for long term then you don't have to pay any taxes on it up to 10 lakhs, but if your profit is more than 10 lakhs then you have to pay tax on it according to your tax slab.

How and why do stock prices change?

There are two types of people in the stock market. Buyers and Sellers. Buyers, people who buy stock,and sellers, people who sell stock. Buyers always want to know,what price the seller is charging for stock and the seller wants to know how much money the buyer is willing to pay for the stock.

Buyers always try to buy stocks at lowest possible price and seller tries to sell stock at a maximum price. So when a stock has more buyers than sellers, its price gets increased,and when there are more sellers than buyers, the price of stock decreases. When stock is bought more, the price rises, and when sold more, the price gets lower.

When investors buy a stock more, its demand increase

s due to which price increases. When investors sell more stocks, then their supply increases,and price decreases.

Assume the stock market is an auction market. What happens in the auction, you have to place bids, and the one who places the highest bid gets the stuff. The same concept is in the stock market. In the stock market if demand is high then the person who pays a higher price will get those shares and the process continues.

And this all happens online, so the online movement moves so fast that the price movement goes on increasing gradually. And you get to see the increasing movement of stock price many times in a single day. It can also happen when there is a high demand for a specific price.

Suppose supply is 10,000 and demand is 1 lakh, which means there are 1 lakh buyers for just 10,000 shares. So the one who pays a high price will get that share. Due to this, many times we get to see that price of a stock increased by one to ten percent within 1 day, 1 week, 1 month, or in just 2 days. If a lot of positive news comes, regarding that stock.

Simultaneously the reverse can also happen if the supply of a stock is high, suppose supply is 10,000 and demand is 1000, which means only 1000 people are willing to buy the share. So what more people will do? They start selling but do not want to buy, because people feel that there is not much power in the stock right now, if any negative news comes regarding the stock. So here the seller has to decrease his price to find buyers, and the price of the share decreases from Rs.100 to Rs.99 and then to 98. Due to this, it may happen that within 1 month or even 1 week, the price of that share will come down by 10%.

So demand and supply depend on what kind of information is coming, positive or negative about the company.

Reason for stock price fluctuations-

Investor sentiments-

The stock performance of a company depends on what the investor thinks about the company. Taking into account the financial statements, reports, media coverage, dividend payout, profit extras, etc. The investors make their negative or positive perceptions about the stock of that company and make their decision on the same basis. If any of the information creates a positive perception for the investor then the share price goes up as the investor buys the stock more, and if the negative perception is formed then the share price goes down as the investor sells the stock more.

Financial institution-

Financial institutions always do very high volume buying and selling of stocks.

Financial Institutions like Mutual Funds, Life Insurance Corporation, etc. are the market's big players. When they buy the stock, the stock price starts to skyrocket and when they start selling the stock, the stock price falls apart like falling leaves. Apart from this, the Indian stock market is very effective with foreign investment. Foreign investment also brings a lot of fluctuations in the market.

Change in political and economic condition-
Political condition-
When the ruling government of the country awakens the people in confidence that good days are coming, then people start spending and investing the money, which increases business profits and the market starts going upwards. On the other hand, if a government fails in the eyes of the people, then people withdraw their investments and keep money with them instead of investing in the market due to which market goes downwards.
Economic condition-
In economic conditions, things like interest rate inflation unemployment, economic growth from microeconomics factors can also lead to the stock market situation. Macro and Micro Economics factors. How are government policies and the overall economy going? How is GDP growth going? How is World Economy going or where our country's company operates, how are those countries performing?

But investors should not be overburdened with the fluctuating price of the stock. It has to be accepted that the stock market is highly volatile. It is better to take advantage of this volatility instead of worrying. Many times, the fundamentally strong stocks are undervalued due to high volatility, just like the market was affected by the coronavirus, due to which many good and fundamentally strong stocks prices fall down, and this is the best time to invest in quality stocks.

Why some shares are expensive and some are not..?

Do you know, the price of one share of Warren Buffett's company Berkshire Hathaway is around Rs.2 crore, so if you want to buy 1 share of this company, then you have to pay around 2 crore rupees.

Suppose that you have to purchase a house, so you went to a colony and there are two plots in the same colony. One is 100 square feet and the other is 400 square feet. Now the first house you are getting for 10 lakhs and the second house you are getting for 40 lakhs. So if you do not have complete information about the house, then what will you think, is that the 10 lakh rupees house is cheap and 40 lakh rupees house is expensive because it is 4 times the price, but the truth is that the second house is 4 times bigger than the first house. This means the price is exactly the same, only there is a difference in size. This means whether you buy 4 houses of 10 lakh rupees or 1 house of 40 lakh rupees it will have the same size in total and cost you the same, the thing is just that in the first case you get 4 small houses and in the second case, you get 1 big house.

In the same way, if a share is of 10 rupees, then you should consider it as a small house and the other one which is of 10,000 rupees, you should consider it as a big house. This means you will have to pay more money for a large share for which you will also get more stake (partnership) in the company and for a small share you will have to pay less money for which you will also get less stake (partnership) in the company.

Companies like MRF, Eicher, Page Industries, etc. did not make so many pieces of their companies. This means they don't make so many shares of less price but they make limited shares of high price, similarly, companies like Ashok Leyland, Tata Motors, etc. make so many shares of their companies of less price.

So that is why the price of one share of some companies is very expensive and the share price of some companies is very less.

Any company can cheapen its stock price whenever it wants, by splitting its shares. For example, the share price of MRF is around 65,000, if the company wants to make its share cheap, it can say that from tomorrow one of our shares will be divided into 10 small pieces. Means one big share of 65000, will divide it into 10 smaller pieces, so now we will get one share for 6500.

So, many companies split their shares to make it cheaper and affordable to people. Like Infosys, which has made its share split many times, if it had not done this split, then the cost of one share of Infosys would be around 1 lakh rupees, but today we get a share of Infosys at the price of 700 to 800 because Infosys has broken its shares many times whenever it gets expensive.

But there are many companies that feel that splitting the shares is not right, so this thing depends from company to company.

.

2 SEBI

SEBI (Securities and Exchange Board of India)
The capital market in India has emerged as a new
sensation since the 1970s. However, along with the
popularity of stock, many corrupt activities have
started to increase. Such as price-fixing, unofficial
private placement, violation of stock exchange rules
and regulations, etc.

So in this situation, the government did decide to
reduce these corrupt activities and to regulate the
Indian stock market, therefore SEBI was set up in
1988 to keep the trust of the people of India in the
stock market. Headquarter of SEBI is located in
Mumbai.

There are around 17 Stock Exchanges operating
currently in India Including NSE&BSE. The
operations of all these stock exchanges are regulated
by SEBI guidelines.

Powers of SEBI-

- SEBI has the power to build the bylaws of the stock exchange and regulate them.
- SEBI has the power to check the accounting books or records of financial intermediaries in India such as stock exchanges, commercial banks, stockbrokers, investment banks, etc.
- SEBI can also prevent the company from listing on any stock exchange.
- SEBI can also handle the registration of stockbrokers.

Objectives of SEBI

The responsibility of SEBI is to ensure that the security market in India function in an orderly manner and providing a healthy in-motion to protect the interest of the investor and the trader and develop the equity market. The main job of SEBI is to protect the corrupt activities in the Indian capital market.

It also takes care of its 3 most important participants.

- The issuer of securities-

This means that the company which is listed on the stock exchange. SEBI also ensures that the allotment of IPO and FPO must be in a transparent and correct way.

- Players in the capital market

The capital market is able to function today because traders and investors exist. Therefore, it is the responsibility of SEBI to ensure that the investor does not become the victim of any fraud or manipulation of the stock market.

- Financial intermediaries

These acts as an intermediate in the security market to ensure that the transaction of the stock market is smooth and secure. SEBI monitors the activities of these stock market intermediaries such as brokers and sub-broker.

Functions of SEBI

SEBI basically carries these three key functions-

- Protective functions

SEBI performs these functions to protect the interest of the Inverters and Financial Institutions from corrupt activities, Such as Price Fixing, Prevention of Insider Trading, Unfair trade practices, etc.

- Regulatory function

With this function, SEBI monitors financial marketing intermediaries and designs guidelines and code of conduct, which also applies to the takeover, Merger, or Amalgamation of the company.

- Development function

One of the SEBI's development functions is to train the intermediaries And to educate investors and aware them of illegal activities of the stock market by using the money from the IEPF (Investor Education and Protection Fund) authority.

The stock market is one of the most important indicators of the country's economic health. If people lose their confidence in the stock market, the number of participants will decrease, so what will happen is that the FDI and FII in the country will also come down which will shake the country's foreign exchange in-flow.

When SEBI was not established, there were a lot of scams and corrupt activities in the stock market, one of which was the famous scam of Harshad Mehta. After SEBI came into power, the stock market activity started becoming more and more transparent. Well, even today some unfavorable activity will happen in the Indian capital market but very rarely. The rules and regulations of the security market are updated from time to time, so SEBI is also becoming strict with its power day by day.

3 BASIC STOCK MARKET TERMS

- Share

For starting any company or for its growth, capital is required, for which small parts of the company are done, to which we call shares and it is sold to the public.

- Support level

In the stock market there is never a deadfall means suddenly a stock reached zero. This never happens. There is always be a scenario where a stock goes down it finds some level and again goes up and it is going up and again down and again up and again down, so what happens whenever a stock goes down to a level, instead of dropping down from there on that point, It is being able to sustain at that level or point, And it bounces back means again goes up from that level or point. So, this is nothing but the support level or price support level. So generally the stock never crashes below that level.

- Resistance level

Similarly, we see a stock goes up and again comes down again goes up and again comes down and again goes up and comes down and so on. So, what is happening is that the stock is going down and is trying to come up but it is not able to cross a specific level or point. It, again and again, goes to that level and comes down but is unable to cross it so this level is called resistance level.

- Portfolio

A stock portfolio groups all the shares you hold. Which shares do we have, how much quantity are there, all this shows us the portfolio.

- Bull market

This is a term used to describe the situation in the market. When the price of the stock is gaining and the investor feels that the rise is going to increase in the coming time, it is called a bull market. Buying of shares get increased in this market.

- Bear market

This is the opposite of the bull market when share prices are falling and the investor feels that the market is going to be bad then it is called a bear market. People feel that the stock price is going to fall further in the coming time. Therefore, the selling of shares in the market gets increased.

- Blue-chip stocks

These are the stocks of reputed companies, which have a good track record in growth and return in the market for a very long time. The risk in these stocks is also slightly less.

- Free float or public float

This means the portion of a company's stock that is held by the public investor.

- Trading session

A trading session means stock market timings. In India, stock markets are closed on weekends and national holidays. Normal trading sessions are timed from 9:15 AM to 3:30 PM, during this time period, you can sell and buy shares.

- Limit order

A limit order means to buy a share at a specific price. If the current price of a share is Rs. 150 and we want to buy it at Rs. 120, then we have to place a limit order of Rs.120, and as soon as the price of that stock comes to Rs. 120 our order will be executed and we will get that stock.

- Market order

When we want to buy a stock at its current market price, we place a market order, the order is executed immediately in the market order.

- Margin

Buying on margin means that we take a loan from a broker to buy shares, with the help of margin trade, we are able to buy more stocks than normal. For this, we need a margin account.

- Volatility

Volatility means how quickly a stock's price moves up and down. More volatile assets are riskier than less volatile assets because it is difficult to predict a stock's price.

- Liquidity

Liquidity means without affecting the price of a share

how easily we can buy that share. A high liquidity share means it can be easily bought and sold.

- Annual report

A company annual report contains the most valuable information about that company. Such as Money Management Strategies, Annual Cash Flow, etc. This report is made so that investors and the public can estimate the value and financial position of the company.

- Average down

There is an approach that investors use to buy more shares when the price of the stock starts falling, which reduces the average price of that share.

If you bought a stock for Rupees 150 and the price of the stock started falling, then you bought the stock again, but this time in rupees 120 and then in rupees 100, then the average price of your investment will be reduced.

- Commodity trading

It is the trading that is carried out on a different platform that has product-related from commerce such as agricultural products, natural resources like oil, metallic sector, etc.

- AMO (After Market Order)

These are the orders which are placed after market closing that is after 3:30 PM. These orders are executed automatically on the next day when the stock market opens i.e. next day at 9.15 AM.

- Assets

Assets are things that earn money for us in the future when we invest some amount in them. Examples are land, stocks, bonds, bank balance, etc.

- Liability

Liabilities are all the things that take money out of our pockets, make us spend, and in which we have no profit in the future. But there is one thing that everyone has liabilities but it is okay to have some liabilities. But remember that, your liabilities should be always less than your assets all the time.

- DII (Domestic institutional investors)

The companies which are based in India i.e. the Indian companies, and if they invest directly in the Indian market, then we call them DII. For Example Domestic Mutual Fund, Domestic Insurance Companies, Domestic Bank, etc. These companies are established in India, they are originated in India and they invest directly in the Indian market.

- FII(Foreign institutional investors)

Those companies who are from outside India and invest in the Indian stock market, we call them FIIs. FII plays a major role in the Indian stock market that is why we should always track the activities of FIIs. These are foreign companies. Examples Euro pacific Growth Fund, the Government of Singapore, Government Pension Fund Global, etc. are some FII.

- ETA(Exchange Traded Funds)

Funds that trade directly on the stock exchange. An ETF is a fund that replicates one of the indexes such as the Nifty or Sensex.

- Small case-

If you don't have time to select good stocks for your portfolio then you can use small case for investing in the stock market without any problem.

With the help of small case, we can easily invest in the stock market. Small case is a basket of stock selected by experts and professionals of the stock market which is made keeping in mind an idea or strategy. Buying a small case is very easy and after buying it, you can also invest in it via SIP.

By using small case we can also add or remove stocks and can also exit partially or completely. Small case is a low-cost, transparent, diversified, and simple approach. There is a Demat account compulsory to invest in the stock market using small case.

4 SHORT SELLING

Those who are beginners in the stock market feel that the only way to earn money in the stock market is to buy the stock at a low price and as the price rises, earn profit by selling it in the stock market. This means we always expect that the price of the stock is going to rise in the future.

But do you know that if the share price is coming down, that is decreasing, you can still earn profit from what we call short selling or shorting or going short.

Short selling is a trading strategy in which the investor first sells stock and later buys it back. Expecting that the stock price will go down.

This is the opposite of the long position in which the investor buys first and then sells later in the hope that the stock price will rise. But in short sell, we, Sell High and Buy Low.

Suppose we have two investors, Sagar & Shyam, who both took their respective positions on ABZ Limited. sagar took a long position and shyam took a short position. ABZ Ltd. Stock has a market price of 100 rupees. Now sagar has bought 10 stocks of this company in which he will invest Rs 1000.

And shyam sold 10 stocks of this company i.e. he did a short sell in which he would sell the investment of Rupees One Thousand.

Now in the first case, let's assume that the price of ABZ Ltd stock falls from Rs 5, that is, now the stock price is Rs 95 and both sagar & shyam close their position, so now when sagar will sell his stocks at Rs 95, then he will have a loss of Rs 50 and as we know that shyam has done short selling so, when he buys the stock at Rupees 95, then he will earn a profit of Rs 50 because he bought stock for Rs 95 and sold it for Rs 100.

In the same way, if the opposite happens, suppose the price for the stock of ABZ Ltd becomes Rs 105, then sagar will have a profit of Rs 50 and shyam has a loss of Rs 50 because he shorted the stock.

Now the question which arises here is that how it is possible that we can sell the stock without buying it already? Because we are not the owner of the stock.

So here we borrow the stock from the broker and only then we are able to sell it and after selling when you buy it back again to complete the trade, then the stock goes back to the broker from whom we had borrowed it. Now when you trade in real-time, it happens in a normal way similarly like buying and selling. According to the availability of the stocks, the transaction completes in seconds.

Short selling is for a slightly advanced trader as it can be a bit risky as in the case of buying your losses are limited whereas in the case of short selling your losses are unlimited. No doubt short selling is an effective way to make money, when the stock price goes down, but keep in mind that always use stop-loss, whether placing a buy order or doing short sell, to reduce risk and losses.

5 STOP LOSS

We have always heard about the profit, but when there is a loss in the market, most of the people do not tell. That is why one must know how to reduce loss.

Stop loss means that you are stopping the loss that is happening in the stock market means that you will not lose any more in the trade you have taken.

Just like when you take a trading position, you take it from the expectation of getting profits, but many times when the situation comes against your expectation then you must leave the trading position at right time to reduce your losses, for this, we use stop loss. Stop loss is nothing but an order or trading position which you use to reduce losses in your actual trading position.

Usually, most people do not put stop-loss after taking a trading position, but when the market suddenly falls, they get a very big loss. That is why it is important to have a stop loss.

Standing without a stop loss in the trading position is like sitting in a sinking boat, to get out of it, you need a lifeboat. Right, stop loss is useful like a lifeboat which you can use to avoid drowning in the stock market. Not taking stop loss will not take much time for your hard-earned money to go away.

Types of stop-loss-

- Primary stop loss

It always remains lower than the purchase price.

This is the most basic type of stop-loss, we put this stop loss at a price lower than the price at which we bought the stock so that if the price of the stock falls below that point, our stock will be sold automatically. And we should not lose more than this. Suppose you have bought a share for Rs 100, so you must put a stop loss below Rs 100 which can be Rs 99, Rs 98, Rs 97, or whatever amount you want. So suppose you put a stop loss at Rs 95 and stock price falls below Rs100 and comes around Rs95 then your stock will automatically be sold at this price even if it falls below Rs95, which means you will only have a loss of Rs5. Similarly, if you do not place stop loss and the stock price keeps falling and you do not leave it at right time then you may bear more loss.

- Trailing stop loss

When we are in profit, we use a trailing stop loss. Trailing stop loss ensures that you always exit with profits. The trailing stop loss changes with the increasing price of stocks. It also increases. As we have seen in the above example we have placed a stop loss at Rs 95 means at below 5 points, similarly here in trailing stop loss we also place a stop loss at Rs95 but here what happens is that, suppose the price of stock increases from Rs100 to Rs102 then our stop loss will also increase by 2 point means now stop loss is Rs97 and if the stock price moves more to Rs105 then stop loss will also move to Rs100.i.e stop loss keeps increasing with the stock price.

The main difference in primary and trailing stop loss is that primary stop loss is fixed at a specific price and trailing stop loss keeps changing with the stock price.

6 HOW TO ANALYZE STOCKS?

Now we will learn to analyze stocks and the things which we must check before selecting stocks to reduce our losses. It is not possible that one must have never faced losses in the stock market, but it is possible to reduce losses by having proper knowledge before selecting stocks.

Market cap-
If you want to buy a company or want to get a hundred percent ownership of a company so how

much money you must have to pay to buy the whole company is known as market cap.

Suppose there is a company XYZ Ltd. whose market cap is one crore rupees, then you have to pay one crore rupees to buy this company completely.

How to calculate market cap

Now we know what market cap is, but how to calculate it, to calculate market cap we need two things, the first value of a share or value of one share of a company and the second total number of shares of that company.

Suppose there is a company ABZ private limited, whose value of 1 share is Rs 1000 and the total number of shares are 10,000 of that company,

now just multiply both the values and you will get the market cap of the company.

Like 1000X10,000=10,000,000.

Value of one share X total number of shares of company = market cap of the company.

So if you have to buy all shares of a company, then how much it will cost, can also be known from the market cap. If the value of a company's stock changes, then its market cap also changes.

The market cap also tells about the size of a company, how big a company is?

Take any stock market company, it falls into one of these three categories.

Small-cap

Mid-cap

Large-cap

The cap means capitalization.

Large-cap companies have a value of more than 75000 crore

Midcap companies have a value between 13000 to 75000 crore

Small-cap companies have a value of less than 13000 crore

These are not specific values these can vary anytime. Any company can become a large-cap from a small-cap or mid-cap and a small-cap from a large-cap or mid-cap. If a small-cap company is having good profit then it can come under large-cap and similarly if a large-cap company is having a loss then it can come under small-cap.

P/E ratio- Price to Earnings ratio-

We need to know a few things before we understand this because in investing many things are related to each other.

Before the P/E ratio, we must know what the EPS ratio is.

EPS is earning per share.

Suppose there is a shop which earns Rs 100 a year.

The shop has four partners and all of them have One-Fourth part.

That means everyone is a partner of 25% in that shop, so if there are 4 shares, all four partners of that shop have one share each and that shop earns a total of Rs 100 means the net profit of that shop is Rupees Hundred. Means profit of one person is Rs25, so this profit per share is known as EPS.

EPS= Company's net profit or total profit
　　　　The number of shares.

Now suppose the value of 1 share of a company ABZ Limited is Rs 1000 and EPS is Rs25, so if I have a share in this company, I will earn Rs25 on that share in a year.

So what does the P/E ratio mean now?
This means, to buy a stock, you are paying how many times of its 1-year earnings.

So suppose, if a company ABZ Limited earns Rs 25 in 1 year or has an EPS of 25 and its share price is also Rs25, then its P/E ratio will be 1, which means you will get the share of that company at the price of its 1-year earnings.
But if ABZ Limited has a share of Rs 1000, so if we divide the value of one share with its EPS, then we will get the PE ratio of that company.

$$P/E = \frac{\text{Value of 1 Share}}{\text{EPS}}$$

So, $\frac{1000}{25} = 40$

So, today you are paying 40 times more to buy the shares of ABZ Ltd. than the earnings of its 1 year.
This means you are paying 40 times more than its EPS value.
Now how do we find out whether a company`s P/E is high or low, whether the stock of that company is expensive or cheap? Should we buy it or not?
So for this, we have to compare the present P/E ratio with two things, one is to check the historic P/E means when it was low and when it was high, and second, the profit growth history of that company in the last few years, means whether the profit of the

company increased or decreased in last few years. (For this we can use a valuation chart of the company which we can get on screener.in website)

Suppose there is a company whose profit has increased rapidly in the last 5 years, even in 3 years, and has also grown rapidly in 1 year, i.e. its profit has improved in the last 5 years and yet its valuation chart shows its P/E ratio has been decreasing.

That is, suppose earlier a company used to run at a P/E of 50 and earns a profit of 10% and now it earns a profit growth of 20%, but now its P/E is 30. So, in such a situation, maybe just by looking at the P/E ratio, we should think whether the company is good or not, it is not completely correct, because as we already know that in investing many things are related with each other.

Remember If P/E is 0 means the company is in a loss and not getting any profit.

Similarly, our whole stock market has its own P/E ratio, seeing that we can estimate how much money and when we should invest.

If we look at the history of the Indian stock market, we will find that the P/E ratio of our stock market (NIFTY and SENSEX)has never been less than 10 nor more than 30, which means the range of the Indian stock market (NIFTY and SENSEX) is 10 to 30, it can be anywhere between this range. Whenever the P/E is around 10, the market has made the bottom and when it has come around 30, it has topped the market, and whenever the market has been around 30 P/E we have seen a big decline in the market from there.

It not only happens in our market, but this thing is also in every stock market, for example, American stock market Dow Jones P/E has never been less than 5 and not more than 35.

Now suppose if Nifty has a P/E of 10, then if you buy the shares of top 50 companies of India in Nifty, and you have invested Rs 10, then you are getting a return of Rs 1 on it. That means you are getting a 10% return on your investment, which is much higher than the interest we get from the bank in our savings account. Similarly, if the Nifty has a P/E of 30, then you will get Rs 1 return after investing Rs 30. Meaning that you are getting about a 3% return on your investment, which is far less than the interest we get from the bank in our saving account.

That is why those who are intelligent investors invest more by analyzing trends and when the Nifty's P/E is low. Similarly, when the Nifty is very high, they invest less.

Enterprise value

Enterprise value is somehow related to market cap, we know that market cap is the price of one share X number of shares.

Enterprise value tells how much the company you are buying will really cost you.

Enterprise value = Market cap – cash + debt (loan)

P/B ratio- Price to book value ratio

P (price) means share price.

Suppose there is a company whose total value is Rupees One Thousand and it only has 2 shares, and both you and your friend are shareholders of that company with 50-50% holding. If that company is sold tomorrow then how many rupees will be your share or how much money you will get? You will get Rupees 500, this is the per-share book value of that company.

Book value= total value of company = 1000   =
Rs500
        Total no. of shares   2

So the book value of that company is Rupees Five Hundred because there are only two shares.

So now, suppose there is a company whose share price is Rs100 and Book Value is Rs300. If that company is sold tomorrow, then every shareholder will get Rs300 per share, which means you will get Rs300 on shares of Rs100, but this is not practically possible because when a company is sold, the expected price is not always received and time taken to sell a company is also very long.

So, you can understand that the company has a cash balance or asset of Rs 300 behind the share of Rs100. This is called the P/B ratio.

P/B ratio = share price = 100 = 0.33
         Book value   300

So you may think that behind Rs100 share, there are assets of Rs300, so the share may be cheaper but the P/B ratio is useful in some industries, not useful in every industry. It is useful in industries such as heavy industry, cement industry, power industry, etc. where capital is used in a hard asset like buying land, building the plant for industry, etc. In these industries, book value is used.

Now suppose there is a software company whose share price is Rs500 and Book Value is Rs100, which means behind the share of Rs500 the company has assets of Rs100. So many of us will think that this stock is very expensive because it has a P/B ratio of 5, but this is not right. As we know, what comes in the book value is things like Machinery, Plant, Vehicle, Factory Furniture, etc.

And as we have seen that this is a software company which does not have such things because a software company can also be started in a room or even in a rented building in which the company does not spend so much on things, so their book value will be less. Things like touch and feel are taken in the book value. So companies that have a strong brand and those who sell on the basis of their brands like IT companies, mobile companies, etc. are not to be judged from the P/B ratio.

Dividend

A company earns whatever profit in a year, out of that profit it decides to distribute some part of its profit to its shareholder. This is Dividend.

Dividend policy
Meaning how much dividend to give, how should it be decided?

Suppose there is a gold mining company that does not have to launch any new product nor have to go to the city and do marketing, then the expenses of this company will not be much in the next two to four years. Also, the company does not have any competitors nor does it have to open any branches in different cities because mining is not done everywhere, so when the company does not have many expenses, then it shares some part of the profit with its shareholders. In such a situation, the dividend yield percentage of that company is higher.

Now suppose there is some big branded company which has to do marketing to maintain its position in the market. New products have to be launched and have to see competition, then the company's expenses increase, then its dividend yield percentage is reduced. So in such a situation, it may be that the company is earning good profit and trying to increase its growth, then the company is good, but the dividend yield percentage is reduced and sometimes it happens if a company is not making any profit or is not growing, even then its dividend yield percentage is low, then it is not right to select the company just by looking at the dividend yield percentage.

Face value of a share

Many years ago, when shares were not digitally processed, the shares were made in physical certificate form or paper printed form, then the amount of shares written on that physical certificate is called face value.

But the face value does not affect the share price. You cannot decide by looking at face value whether the share is expensive or cheap, many times it is that the price of a share is higher than its face value and sometimes the price of a share is lower than its facial value.

Never use face value for share selection. The face

value is such that 10 grams of silver is of Rs300 but 10 grams of gold is of Rs30,000, but both are not the same, their value and quality are different, so the face value of a share does not matter by being expensive and cheap. The thing which matters is that whether the company is growing or not.

Face value only tells how many pieces of a company have been done. Suppose there is a company that issues shares of Rs 1000, which means that the company has issued 100 shares of Rs 10 face value, or if the company wanted, then it will issue 1000 shares with Rs 1 Face Value. That is why face value is useful for share division only.

Promoter holding

Promoter holding means how many percent of shares a company's owner holds in the company, that is, how many shares does promoter or the owner of the company own.

This shows how much the owner trusts his company, if promoter holding in a company is above 45% then it is a good thing but at the same time we also have to see that whether promoter holding stocks are not to be pledged, because many promoters may have pledged their shares if they do not have money to run the company.

So also see if promoter shares are pledged anywhere.

Many times some company has promoter holding zero or less than 45%. This happens only in a professionally managed company, i.e. a company with many owners or a company that is running by many different companies, then such company has less promoter holding.

Also, the promoter holding of a bank is not more

than 25% because of RBI's restriction i.e. a promoter cannot hold more than 25% in a bank so that no single person has all power to run the bank or to ruin. Also, we should see whether the promoter's holdings are decreasing or increasing in the last few years.

Net margin or PAT margin (profit after tax)
Selling price – cost price – expenses.
The remaining profit is called Net margin.
Mark up
Meaning at how much cost are you selling by increasing the price of something.
It uses cost price or depends on the cost price
Profit margin
Out of the selling price how much are my expenses.
Selling Price - Expenses = profit margin.
It depends on the selling price.

ROE (return on equity)
Suppose you have to start a business and need money, so if you start a business by applying money yourself or taking money from friends and relatives and in return give them shares in the business. It is called equity. Debt- when you take a loan from people or banks on interest. It is called debt.

Suppose you took money for business from your friends and relatives, and together you got the Rs1000 that you put in the business and in return, you gave shares to your friends and relatives and after 1 year of business you earned Rs1200. You made a profit of Rs200 on Rs1000, it is called Return on Equity. How much money you had invested in the business at the beginning of the year, and how much money you made on that money in a year, tells us ROE.

The purpose of any business is to earn as much money as possible by applying or investing a little money.

Debt to equity ratio

The ideal debt to equity ratio must be always zero or around zero.

Now suppose there is a person. He started his business and raised 100% money from his friends and relatives in the business, which means he created equity capital, and there is another person who took 50% of the money for the business from friends, relatives, and the other 50% he took a loan from the bank or from anyone.

Now suppose for some reason the profit in both the company was reduced or not got any profit, now in such a situation, the first person who started a company with 100% Equity Capital, that is, he gave shares to people in exchange for money and the company is not yet profitable. If it is happening, it may be that for some time, the shareholder also does not get any benefit, but the company will keep running.

At the same time, the other person who started the company on a 50% loan and the company is not in profit right now, but the company has to repay the loan, whether the company has money or not or if the company is in profit or not and in such a way if the company remains in a loss for a long time and does not have money left to pay the loan, then the company sinks.

That is why we always have to see whether the debt-equity ratio is as low as possible or around zero.

But you must never see this ratio in any bank's stock because the job of the bank is to take money from people in the form of RD, in the form of FD and further lending to someone else on loan, that's why debt-equity ratio must not be seen in any finance company or bank.

How to know if a company or its management is good or not?

If you invest long-term in a company's stock, then it is important to see how the management of that company or the people who are handling the company, it means that the management of that company thinks about its investors and shareholders or not. So that you can decide the company is safe to invest in or not.

The commitment of management-

Now how to find out whether the management who commits to his investors and shareholders, fulfills the commitment or not. The way is that every company declares its quarterly results and together it also provides guidance in which it is given that what are the future plans of the company. How much growth the company is expecting in the coming time, how much profit the company is expecting, what challenges will the company have in the future, all these things are given in that guidance.

Now suppose the quarterly result of a company has come and written in its guidance about all future plans and profits of the company, but we do not know whether the management is telling the truth or can be false to increase the value of its shares. So if he is speaking like this, then what you have to do is look at the result of the last seven-eight quarters and the guidance provided with them at that time by the company and read it and check its result in its coming quarters.

Now suppose, now December 2017 is going on, then you have to see the quarterly results of the company's January 2016 to March 2016 and the guidance of that time, in which that company has said to earn profit in the coming quarters or the vision of that company and what company said about all these things, so study all these things and in the coming time, check the commitment of the company on the basis of the results posted by the company.

When you look at the previous results, you will know that the management is fulfilling its promises made in the past or just misleading its shareholders and investors.

Now the guidance details of the large-cap or big companies, you will also know through the news channel or newspaper. But for those small companies, you will have to use Google or use an app or website like Money control, ET Money, or you will get all the information on the website of NSE India.

Debt on company
The company whose management is continuously reducing or trying to reduce its debt or loan, means that management is good. He cares about the money

of his shareholder and investor. But if the company which has more loans will have to pay more interest and the company which will give more interest will have less profit and when the profit is less, then the growth of that company will be less and that stock will come down and won't perform well in coming time.

Promoter stake or holding

If the management or promoter of the company that is running the company, increase their stake in the company, means the person who is running that company is confident that in the coming time our company can grow better, and instead of this, if the promoters are continuously selling their stake, then it means that something negative in the company is going on, the news of which has not come out but the management of the company knows about it because if all is going well in the company then no promoter will reduce their holdings.

From these points, you can know how the management of a company is.

7 ANALYSIS OF BANKING STOCKS

What to check before picking banking stocks?

CASA ratio (current account plus savings account

ratio)

This means how much current account plus savings account are in a bank.

A bank has many deposit accounts Like FD, Current Account, RD, Savings Account, Different Bank Funding, etc. from which deposits have been collected in the bank, out of these deposits account, how much is the percentage of current and saving accounts, this information is known from CASA ratio.

This is necessary because the current account has 0% interest and the savings account gets around 4% interest or below, and this is the money that the bank gets very cheaply. That is why many new banks want that they have a maximum current account and saving account because they have to pay less interest on these accounts when compared to FD, RD, etc.

That is why banks initially give more interest on the savings account and then gradually reduce the interest when the bank gets well established.

CASA ratio shows how much money the bank has on which it does not have to pay much interest because if a bank has more FD accounts, then it will have to pay 7-8% interest on them and if the money from that FD account is given to someone on loan for 12-13% interest, then the bank is earning only 4-5% on that money.

But if a bank has savings account money on which bank gives 3-4% interest and lends it to someone for a loan at 12-13 %, then the bank will earn around 8% from that money.

That is why, if the CASA ratio percentage of a bank is

high, then it is a very good stock because the more established bank the more the percentage of CASA ratio.

NPA (non-performing asset)

Meaning if a bank has given a Rs1000 Loan, then how much is the percentage of money that has not been returned?

Because banking business is the business of giving loans, the bank that is good at identifying that who will borrow money and will repay it, and who will borrow money and will not repay it. That bank is automatically the best because it will give a loan after a complete investigation. Most of the time we should consider this (NPA) to be less than 1 to 2% or as less as possible.

Cost of fund or cost of liabilities

This ratio tells us how much total interest a bank has to pay on the money that the bank has in the form of a current account, saving account, FD, RD, etc.

With this, whenever you check the CASA ratio, also check how much the cost of liabilities or cost of funds percentage of that bank is and it should be between 4-5% or as low as possible.

Advanced growth or loan growth %

This tells us how many loans the bank has distributed this year as compared to last year.

Suppose a bank had distributed loans of Rs1000 last year and this year it has advanced growth or loan growth of 10%, this means that at present, bank's Rs1100 are given in the form of loan and because the bank gives loan and take interest on it, then this percentage tells us how much the growth of that bank is.

The better this percentage the good it is, but it is not difficult for a bank to increase loan growth %, because many people are ready to take a loan and the bank can give loan no matter how much people want, but the bank also has to see that the one who took the loan, will he repay it or not, and how much money the bank has with it to give the loan.

That is why we have to see two more ratios with loan growth %. One is the NPA percentage which must be as low as possible and the other is CAR (Capital Adequacy ratio).

CAR (Capital adequacy ratio)-

It tells us how much money the bank already has with it. The higher the CAR percentage, the better it is. The more this ratio means the more money a bank has. This ratio should only be more than 13-14% normally. The higher this ratio is, the bank will be able to give loans easily and faster. But increasing this ratio is a bit difficult for the bank because the more the bank has deposit accounts, the more money will be there and the more CAR percentage will be.

The Beginner`s Stock

8 BASIC TRADING STRATEGY

Everyone has their own trading style. Trading has a lot of different strategies, some basic strategies are mentioned below.

- **Trend Following**- trends are everywhere, even in the stock market. In the stock market, some sectors become active due to changes in news, coverage, and laws. That is, they come in trend means get highlighted. So the traders who follow the trend try to follow the news coverage, different information regarding the stock, and then trade with that momentum. For ex – suppose the govt. reduced tax on the raw material used for making garments, due to which the garment company also reduced prices of its product and starts manufacturing more products and its sales also increases as people start purchasing more and more products of the company, due to this the company comes in trend for a while and its stock price also increases, as people see growth in the company.

- **Scalping-**Scalping is a trading method in which a trader trades continuously and tries to make money from small gains. It is based on quantity rather than quality. This strategy is not very profitable for new traders. In this trading, the trader continuously buys and sells stocks and tries to earn profit from small transactions.

- **Price action**-With this style of trading, you specifically see the price movement of the stock. This means giving importance to a big percentage volume of stock, looking for it, and making the decision based on the price movement instead of fundamentals. In this, the trader actually tries to find out high buy or sell volume in stock means which companies stock is buying or selling more.

- **Range trading**-In range trading, a trader relies on support and resistance to set the buy and sell point. Support means stopping stock from falling below a specific level and Resistance means stopping stock from crossing a specific level.

The Beginner's Stock

9 MUTUAL FUNDS

There are two types of funds- active funds and passive funds.

Active funds

The fund manager actively manages the active fund, they analyze the individual company and industries and then decide himself which shares are good to invest in. Fund managers keep actively managing the active funds. That is why their expense ratio is high. That is, in exchange for managing your fund, fund managers charge some fees which is around 1-2%, this is known as the expense ratio.

That is, if the expense ratio of an active fund is 2% and you invest Rs1000 in it, then that mutual fund will deduct 2% of your total investment annually. The 2 percent of Rs1000 is Rs 20, which means the mutual fund company (AMC) will charge you Rs20 annually in exchange for managing your fund.

A mutual fund is a good example of an Active fund.

Mutual means two or more people and funds means money. So, when two or more people invest money for the same objective, it is called a Mutual Fund.

The objective of a mutual fund is to earn profit from the market i.e. from equity and debt.

Many people want to earn money from the market, but they have neither time nor proper knowledge, in such a situation, they go to an AMC (Asset Management Company). Companies that manage the fund are called AMC, for Example, ICICI Prudential

AMC, SBI Mutual Fund, Motilal Oswal AMC, etc.
So that AMC appoints a Mutual Fund Manager who
is a qualified and knowledgeable person who tries to
earn profit by investing money in the market i.e.
Stocks, Bonds, Treasury Bills, Corporate deposits, etc.
on behalf of these investors.

Every Mutual Fund has an investment objective that
depends on its risk-taking capacity i.e. risk is high or
low and the investment is being made for how long.
Example 1Year, 3 Years, 5 Years, etc.

Basic Types of Mutual Funds-
Equity, Debt and Balance.
In Equity mutual funds, your money is invested in the
stock market. It`s   for aggressive investors   who
want to take more risk and earn more profit.

In debt mutual funds, your money is invested in
Government Security, Treasury Bills etc. Debt is
for conservative investors who want to take less risk a
nd prefer to stay on safe side. In this risk is low so the
profit ratio is also less.

Balanced mutual fund is for investors who want a mix
ture or hybrid of both equity and debt.
Some mutual fund schemes are like bluechip fund, reg
ular saving fund, gold fund etc.
We can invest in mutual funds in two ways.

Lumpsum or one time, means investing your money t
ogether at one time.

SIP (systematic investment plan) means invest some amount regularly every month or every quarter. Nowadays we can start SIP from Rs100 also.

Passive funds-

Passive funds are not actively managed. Index funds are a good example of passive funds. What an index fund does is invest in different indices, which are Sensex, Nifty, and others. These are all indices, so if there is a nifty index fund, then those funds will invest your money in the Nifty. Investment is done according to the weightage of stocks listed in Nifty.

Suppose, Nifty Fifty has a total of 50 stocks, in which HDFC Bank has been given a weightage of 10.7%, Reliance has been given a weightage of 9.9%, Infosys has given a weightage of 6.4% and similarly different companies have been given different weightage.

So whatever money you invest in Nifty's index fund, 10.7% of the money will be invested in HDFC Bank stock, 9.9% of the money will be invested in Reliance's stock and similarly, the rest of the money will also be invested in different stocks. So, the job of an index fund is to track the performance of these indices.

The returns that an index (like Nifty or Sensex) is offering, the same returns we get through index funds.

For example, if nifty is offering a 15% return then we will also get a 15% return by investing in a nifty index fund.

Index funds do not have to actively manage, hence their expense ratio is very low, which is around 0.1 %, so the expense ratio of index funds is almost nil.

Index funds come in two types of formats.

ETF format and normal format.

To buy an ETF fund, you must have a demat account. We cannot do SIP in ETF Index Fund.

To buy a normal index fund we don't need demat account, normal index funds can be purchased in the similar way we purchase mutual funds. We can do SIP in Normal Index Fund.

NAV (Net asset value)

Mutual Funds scheme has units in the same way as a company has shares and just as the price of a share is known from its share price, similarly, the price of a unit is known from its NAV.

Let us assume that there is a mutual fund scheme called ABZ mutual fund, whose NAV is Rupees 10 i.e. the price of one unit is Rs10. So, If you invest in Rs1000 in ABZ Mutual Fund, then you will get 1000 units of ABZ Mutual Fund, so next year, if the NAV of ABZ Mutual Fund rises from 10 rupees to 12 rupees and if you sell your 100 units at the NAV of Rs12 then after selling your unit you will get Rs1200. This means you will get a 20% profit on your investment.

Exit load

Usefully, it is a fine of 0.5 to 2% which you have to pay when you sell an equity-based mutual fund before 1 year. It is only applicable to equity mutual funds. But if you sell your mutual fund investments after 1 year then you don't have to pay any exit load. Except in tax saving-based mutual funds because they have a minimum lock-in period of 3 years.

The Beginner`s Stock

10 DIFFERENT OPTIONS AVAILABLE FOR INVESTMENT IN INDIA OTHER THAN STOCKS.

You must have always heard that if we reduced monthly expenses from our monthly earnings then our monthly savings will come.

Earnings – expenses = savings

But according to the most successful investor Warren Buffett, it should be like this, reduce monthly savings from monthly earnings then our monthly expenses will come, so this means that we should first invest some part of our unspent money on a monthly basis.

Earnings – savings = expenses.

One Thing to Notice is that we get returns on investment has a positive relation with risk. The higher the risk, the greater the chance of getting higher returns on the investment.

PPF (public provident fund)

PPF is considered the best and secured long-term investment option in India, which is also completely tax-free. It is fully guaranteed by the Central Government of India. We can open a PPF account in any bank or post office. In this, we can deposit from Rs 500 to Rs 1.5 Lakhs every year. Either together or on a monthly basis and we have to do this for 15 years which is its lock-in period after 15 years, we can get it extended for another 5 years. The interest rate you get in it is 8 to 9 percent.

Its first advantage is that it gets a triple E exemption. Triple E means exempt, exempt, exempt means that in PPF we get tax exemption from our investment amount, rate of interest, and the income that is received on maturity is also exempted from tax. The second advantage is that we also get a loan facility in it. Investors can also avail loans from the third year to six year on the basis of the investment.

Liquid mutual fund

Liquid funds are a type of mutual funds, in which there is no risk of having loss. Every money you invest, it always grows. One advantage of this is that you can withdraw the money invested in it at any time because there is no lock-in period. Its main disadvantage is that we get less interest, which is around 6-7%, when compared to different stocks or mutual funds.

This fund is also used like the bank's alternative because you can deposit and withdraw money in this fund at any time.

Real estate investment

In this, we buy the property, land, building, etc. and after some time sells it at a high price and the profit we get is called capital gains. The real estate industry is on rapid growth in India. It has a huge prospect on all the big sectors. Such as housing, commercial, manufacturing, etc. For individual investors, it may be the best option to buy a flat or plot. Real estate is also called the money-making industry in India. It gives us

30 to 100% guaranteed returns. But to earn such a high profit, the investor should do proper research and only then buy any property. The most probable place where the price is going to increase in the next 5 to 10 years.

Gold

Gold is an Evergreen investing product because it always has liquidity. We can invest in gold in many formats.

Gold deposit scheme, gold ETF, gold bar, gold mutual fund, digital gold, etc.

Gold deposit scheme offers three to five percent interest. Which is tax-free, and there is a locking period of 3 to 5 years. In this, we get gold bonds in exchange for gold. At maturity, the investor can take gold or cash according to his preference.

Digital gold
It is similar to purchasing gold only here you purchase gold in digital form which is stored in a digital locker you can also get digital gold delivered at your home in a physical form whenever you want.

In this, you can start investing from as low as rupees 1.

We can invest in digital gold by using Paytm, phonepe, etc.

Where we can purchase gold at market price and when the market price of gold increases, our investment amount also increases.

Post office saving scheme

Post office saving scheme because it is a government saving scheme, it has a very low risk and has a medium rate of interest. There are some popular post office saving scheme like National Saving Certificate scheme, Recurring Deposit, Senior Citizen Saving Scheme, etc.

National Savings Certificate Scheme is the best option among all these, with guaranteed returns if you don't want to take any type of risk.

Together it is very helpful for those who want to save tax. It has a locking period of 5 years and 10 years only. In this, you can start investing only with Rs100 and there is no limit of the maximum amount. Whatever interest you get in it is also tax-free.

Companies FD

Company FD is preferred as compared to bank FDs because it has a high-interest rate. The company uses these FDs in order to borrow money from small investors, the investment period for this type of FD should be carefully selected because the investor cannot withdraw his money before the maturity date, as in a bank FD. These company FDs are not under any insurance benefit and these instruments do not have RBI control, so there is little risk as compared to Bank FD, that's why it has a higher interest rate.

Bonds

A bond is a type of financial instrument that shows that the company has money on borrowings that it has to repay to its bondholders. Bonds are generally issued by Government Agencies, Financial institutions, etc.

Bonds are more secure than stocks and have higher interest rates compared to bank.

11 CONCLUSION

If you want to invest in the stock market, keep in mind one thing, if you are able to select the company yourself, then only invest in the stock market. To invest in the stock market, you have to learn how the company is chosen. What kind of analysis is to be done? If you are not interested in learning all these things and you want things ready-made, you should go for Mutual Funds.

So if you are not ready to learn and you feel that it is not your job to select the company or you will not be able to do it, then do not invest in the stock market. Better to invest in mutual funds where qualified fund managers manage your fund, where you do not have to think about which company to invest in and which not.